CONTENTS

COOL DIGGING MACHINES!   4

BIG: Bucket-wheel excavator   6

SMALL: Micro excavator   8

TALL: Dragline excavator   10

WIDE: Tunnel boring machine   12

HIGH: High-reach excavator   14

HEAVY: Mining shovel   16

LIGHT: Amphibious excavator   18

LONG: Long-reach excavator   20

TOUGH: Chain trencher   22

FUN: Diggerland   24

TEN MORE COOL FACTS   26

STACK UP THOSE STATS!   28

QUIZ   28–29

GLOSSARY   30

FURTHER INFORMATION   31

INDEX AND ANSWERS   32

Words in **bold** can be found in the glossary on pages 30–31.

COOL DIGGING MACHINES!

Here are ten of the coolest digging machines you'll ever see! But they're not just awesome to look at. They're cool because they're monstrously massive, extra-long or can chew through the hardest ground.

Digging machines work in all sorts of places. They have to be made of hard, tough steel to survive in **quarries**, **construction sites** and in wet and muddy places. They dig and shift tonnes of material. And they have cool equipment, such as giant buckets, powerful claws and wide **tracks**.

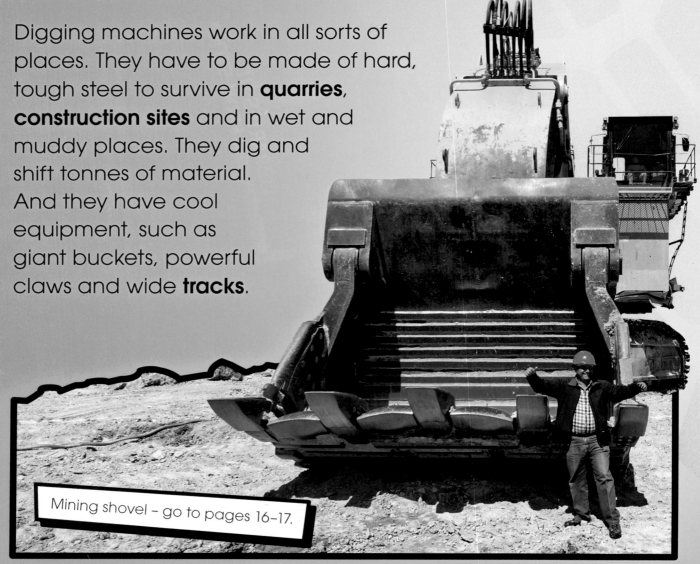

Mining shovel – go to pages 16–17.

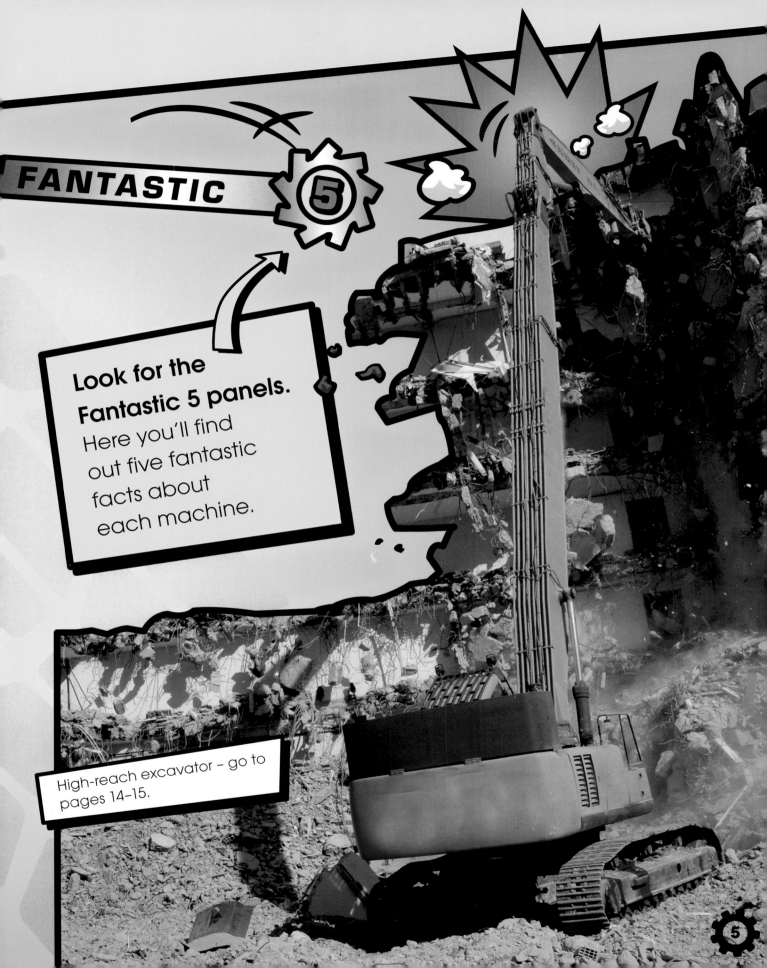

FANTASTIC 5

Look for the Fantastic 5 panels. Here you'll find out five fantastic facts about each machine.

High-reach excavator – go to pages 14–15.

BIG

BUCKET-WHEEL EXCAVATORS are the biggest digging machines ever built. These machines rule as they slowly chomp through the earth.

In just one day, the 21 buckets that spin around on *Bagger 293's* 21-metre-wide wheel can dig out an amazing 220,000 tonnes of **coal**. The buckets drop the coal onto a **conveyor belt**, which takes the material from the front to the back of the excavator.

BAGGER 293

- ⚙ **Height:** 96 metres
- ⚙ **Weight:** 14,200 tonnes
- ⚙ **Length:** 225 metres
- ⚙ **Speed:** 1 kilometre per hour
- ⚙ **Number of crew:** 5

BOOM
The boom is another name for the arm of an excavator.

TRACKS
A big excavator has wide, metal tracks instead of wheels to stop it sinking into the ground. Bagger 293 has 12 sets of tracks.

SMALL

Not all cool machines are big. MICRO EXCAVATORS are perfectly designed to dig in the smallest of spaces.

Need to dig a tiny trench? The *Kubota K008-3's* smallest bucket is just 15 centimetres (cm) wide. But don't let this tiny machine fool you. Micro excavators are tough enough to work on rugged building sites. A special pedal kicks the digger up a **gear** so it can whiz off to the next mini-digging job.

BREAKER
Instead of a bucket, a small breaker can be attached to the end of the boom to smash up tough concrete and rocky ground.

ADJUSTABLE
The K008-3 has adjustable rubber tracks, so it can fit through a doorway or a gate that is just 70 cm wide.

FANTASTIC

5

Kubota K008-3

⚙ **Weight:** 1 tonne
⚙ **Length:** 2.5 metres
⚙ **Speed:** 2–4 kilometres per hour
⚙ **Track type:** Rubber
⚙ **Digging depth:** 1.7 metres

TALL

With a boom long enough for a sprinter to set a world record on, a DRAGLINE EXCAVATOR drags loads over huge distances.

These strange-looking excavators are **mining** experts that work a bit like a giant fishing rod. The super-tall *Caterpillar 8750* has a large bucket on the end of a cable that swings away from the boom. The bucket is dragged towards the machine, scooping up its load as it goes.

FANTASTIC

Caterpillar 8750

⚙ **Height:** 84 metres

⚙ **Weight:** 7,500 tonnes

⚙ **Boom length:** 132 metres

⚙ **Digging depth:** 78 metres

⚙ **Engine type:** 30 electric motors (1,250–1,650 **horsepower** each)

FEET
Dragline excavators don't move on steel tracks. Huge feet 'walk' the machine across the quarry floor.

BIG MUSKIE
A dragline excavator nicknamed 'Big Muskie' has the biggest bucket ever built. The bucket weighs 208 tonnes and can hold two buses.

WIDE

There's nothing a TUNNEL BORING MACHINE (TBM) can't dig through! These wide machines slowly spin around to carve out tunnels deep underground.

TBMs are used to dig tunnels through mountains, below cities and even under the seabed. A cutting plate covered with thousands of teeth slowly spins and grinds away at the rock. TBMs measure from 1 metre to 17.5 metres wide. The biggest one in the world is nicknamed 'Bertha'.

FANTASTIC

5

'BERTHA'

⚙ **Weight:** 6,100 tonnes

⚙ **Length:** 99 metres

⚙ **Width:** 17.5 metres

⚙ **Speed:** Took over four years to dig a 2.8-kilometre-long tunnel in Seattle, USA

⚙ **Price:** £64 million

CONCRETE

The TBM also makes tunnel walls as it works. Wet **concrete** can be sprayed from the sides of the machine or ready-made sections of dry concrete are slid into place to form the tunnel walls.

SECTION

Each section of the TBM is lowered into a hole in the ground and connected to the next section.

HIGH

Some excavators don't dig things up. The HIGH-REACH excavator is all about tearing things down!

High-reach excavators can demolish buildings up to 40 metres high. On the end of the arm is a huge claw that pulls the building down piece by piece. One of the biggest high-reach excavators works in New Zealand. It is nicknamed *'Twinkle Toes'*.

CRUSHER
The massive claw on the end of the arm is known as a crusher. Twinkle Toes' crusher is one of the biggest in the world.

FANTASTIC 5

TWINKLE TOES (LIEBHERR 984)

- ⚙ **Weight:** 220 tonnes
- ⚙ **Boom length:** 65 metres
- ⚙ **Width:** 5.2 metres
- ⚙ **Power:** 675 horsepower
- ⚙ **Crusher claw:** 2.5 metres wide

FOG
The FOG is the Falling Object Guard. This cage protects the driver in the cab from getting squashed by falling rubble!

HEAVY

Monster MINING SHOVELS work in mines and quarries. They are super-strong so they can dig and lift thousands of tonnes of rock and coal.

The massive bucket on the end of the boom can shift more than 75 tonnes of rocks in one scoop. That's a lot of rock! These **hydraulic** excavators have to be very strong and heavy to lift all that weight without tipping over. The *Caterpillar 6120B H FS* weighs a massive 1,270 tonnes.

Caterpillar 6120B H FS

⚙ **Cab height:** 12 metres

⚙ **Track height:** 3.2 metres

⚙ **Engine power:** 4,500 horsepower

⚙ **Digging depth:** 3 metres

⚙ **Bucket size:** 65 m^3

TEETH
The big steel teeth on the bucket wear down quickly. They can be unbolted and replaced with new ones.

BUDDY UP
Mining shovels buddy up with quarry dump trucks. These big trucks take away the rock and coal that the shovel digs up.

LIGHT

Some diggers can even swim! The *Caterpillar/EIK* **AMPHIBIOUS** EXCAVATOR makes light work of digging deep in rivers and **harbours**.

The top half of an amphibious excavator is the same as a normal digger. But underneath, two huge air-filled floats stop the digger sinking underwater. These cool machines can dig up mud and sand where no other excavator can reach.

PONTOONS

The air-filled floats are called pontoons. Even though they are made of thick, heavy steel, there is so much air in them that they float easily in water.

FANTASTIC

5

Caterpillar/EIK

⚙ **Weight:** Up to 40 tonnes

⚙ **Length:** 12 metres

⚙ **Width:** 7.3 metres

⚙ **Airtight compartments:** 6 (3 in each pontoon)

⚙ **Digging depth:** 12 metres

DREDGING

Digging up sand and mud from underwater is called dredging.

LONG

Sometimes it's really useful to have an extra-long arm. LONG-REACH excavators can get to places that other excavators can't.

Long-reach excavators can work in tough terrain, including giant quarries and large building sites. The *Hitachi Zaxis 870 LCH-3* even works next to rivers or the sea to reach and dig deep down underwater without getting its tracks wet. The boom on this machine has to be super-strong to be so long.

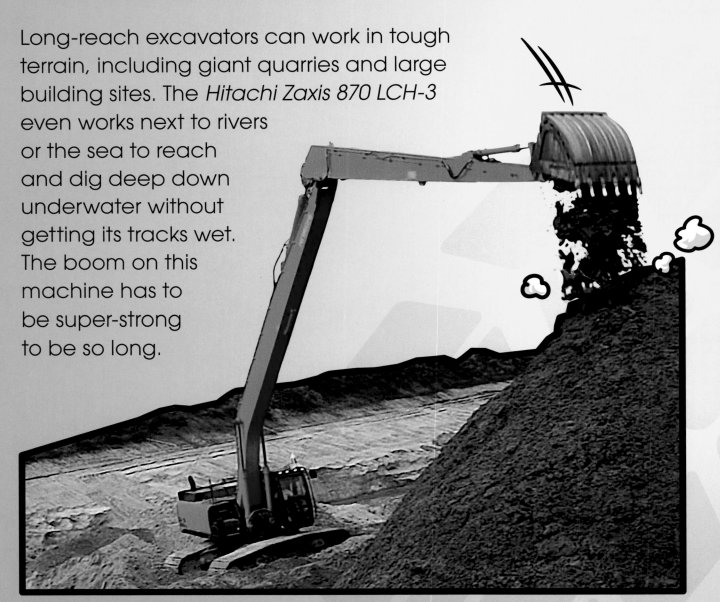

HITACHI ZAXIS 870 LCH-3

⚙ **Weight:** 84 tonnes

⚙ **Boom length:** Around 12 metres (but some are **custom-built** to be 45 metres long!)

⚙ **Speed:** 4 kilometres per hour

⚙ **Engine type:** Diesel

⚙ **Engine power:** 532 horsepower

COUNTERWEIGHT
The heavy body of the machine acts as a counterweight, so the machine won't tip over when the boom is fully extended.

Argentinosaurus

NECK
The boom can be as long as the neck of some of the biggest and longest dinosaurs ever discovered!

TOUGH

A CHAIN TRENCHER looks like a massive chainsaw attached to a digger, or even to the back of a truck. These tough **armoured** machines chew through just about anything – even frozen soil!

The *PZM-3* trencher digs trenches for cables or pipes. It can also work in **reverse** and fill in trenches, too. This trencher folds down from the back of a truck or digger, so these machines can go just about anywhere.

FANTASTIC

5

PZM-3

⚙ **Built especially for:**
Ukrainian army

⚙ **Temperature range:** 40ᶜ to -40ᶜ

⚙ **Digging depth:** 1.2 metres

⚙ **Trench width:** 0.9 metres

⚙ **Digging speed:** 300–400 metres per hour

CONVEYOR BELT
The trencher doesn't use buckets to move the soil. The soil drops straight onto a conveyor belt and is thrown out of the back of the machine.

HANDHELD
The military use smaller, handheld trenchers to help them build camps in very remote locations.

FUN!

Diggers don't only do lots of hard work. The diggers at DIGGERLAND THEME PARKS have a fun side, too!

Have you ever wanted to drive a digger? At Diggerland you can do just that on full-sized diggers. Put on your hard hat and get behind the controls in the cab to dig up mounds of soil like a real construction worker, or whiz around on *SPINDIZZY.*

SPINDIZZY

⚙ **Machine type:** JCB JS220L

⚙ **Weight:** 26 tonnes

⚙ **Number of riders:** 8

⚙ **Minimum height of rider:** 1 metre

⚙ **Cost:** £155,000

THEME PARK
There are digger theme parks in the UK and the USA where you can have a lot of digger fun.

STUNT DRIVING
It's not all about digging. You can watch JCB stunt driving and digger racing, and have a go at dumper driving.

TEN MORE COOL FACTS

BIG: The word 'bagger' is German for 'excavator'. **BAGGER 293** was made by a German company called TAKRAF.

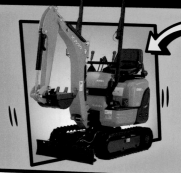

SMALL: A **KUBOTA K008-3's** engine produces a tiny 10 horsepower.

TALL: A **CATERPILLAR 8750** dragline uses four of its motors to 'walk' and eight of its motors to drag its load along the quarry floor.

WIDE: **BERTHA** is programmed to play a tune inside the machine to keep workers entertained!

HIGH: **TWINKLE TOES** got its name after a New Zealand radio station, More FM, ran a competition to name the machine.

HEAVY: The bucket on a **CATERPILLAR 6120B H FS** is so big it takes only four bucket-loads to fill up a dump truck.

LIGHT: Amphibious excavators are often moved in pieces and then put together on site. It takes a four-person team three hours to assemble a **CATERPILLAR/EIK** Amphibious excavator.

LONG: The controls in the cab of a **HITACHI ZAXIS 870 LCH-3** have a power boost button to release extra power in tough digging conditions.

TOUGH: **PZM-3** comes equipped with a remote control system, so in risky situations it can be operated remotely.

FUN: There are 18 different rides at Diggerland. **SPINDIZZY** is one of the most popular rides.

STACK UP THOSE STATS!

Here are the ten cool machines with all their stats and a few more. Which is your favourite?

	Bagger 293	Kubota K008-3	Caterpillar 8750	'Bertha'
Weight	14,200 tonnes	1 tonne	7,500 tonnes	6,100 tonnes
Height	96 metres	2.2 metres	84 metres	17.5 metres
Length	225 metres	2.5 metres	23 metres	99 metres
Boom length	225 metres	3 metres	132 metres	
Top speed	1 kph	2–4 kph	less than 1 kph	1.3 kp year
Width		70 centimetres	23 metres	17.5 metres
Crew	5	1		600
Digging depth	25 metres	1.7 metres	78 metres	As deep underground as needed!
Engine type	Electric power	Diesel	30 electric motors	Electric power
Engine power		10 hp	1,250–1,650 hp each	
Track type	Steel	Rubber	Steel 'walking' feet	
Bucket size	15 m³		116 m³	
Price	£800 million			£64 million

Caterpillar 8750 is the most powerful machine.

'Bertha' is the slowest machine.

QUIZ

1 What is the word we use for an excavator's arm?

2 What can a micro excavator fit through?

3 How do dragline excavators move about?

4 How long did it take Bertha to dig a tunnel?

5 What is the name of the high-reach excavator on page 14?

	'Twinkle Toes'	Caterpillar 6120B H FS	Caterpillar/EIK	Hitachi Zaxis 870 LCH-3	PZM-3	'Spindizzy'
	220 tonnes	1,270 tonnes	40 tonnes	84 tonnes	17.5 tonnes	26 tonnes
	5 metres	12 metres		5.2 metres		3 metres
		16 metres	12 metres	13.5 metres		9.5 metres
	65 metres			12–45 metres		5.7 metres
		2 kph		4 kph	100 kph	6 kph
	5.2 metres	9.6 metres	7.3 metres	4.5 metres	90 centimetres (trench width)	3.3 metres
	1	1	1	1	10	1
		3 metres	12 metres	5 metres	1.2 metres	6 metres
	Diesel	Diesel	Diesel	Diesel	Diesel	Diesel
	675 hp	4,500 hp		532 hp	400 hp	173 hp
	Steel	Steel	Plastic	Steel	Steel	Steel
		65 m^3		4.3 m^3		
						£155,000

PZM-3 is the fastest machine.

kph = kilometres per hour   m^3 = cubic metres   hp = horsepower

6 What can be taken off and put on digging buckets?

7 Which kind of digger can float?

8 Why does a long-reach excavator's boom have to be super-strong?

9 What does a chain trencher look like?

10 How tall do you have to be to ride on Spindizzy at Diggerland?

GLOSSARY

amphibious a machine that is able to work both on land and in water

armoured covered with strong metal plates

coal a black or dark brown rock that is burned to make electricity in power stations

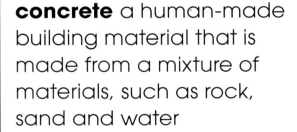

concrete a human-made building material that is made from a mixture of materials, such as rock, sand and water

construction site another name for a building site

conveyor belt a long machine that moves material from one place to another

custom-built made to order

gear one of a set of cogs inside an engine that makes a machine move faster or slower, depending on which gear is chosen

harbour a natural or human-made place along the coast where ships and boats can shelter from rough waves

horsepower a measure of how much power an engine produces

hydraulic when machines use liquid, such as oil, under high pressure to power pieces of equipement

military to do with the army, navy, airforce or other armed forces

mining digging in a quarry for materials, such as coal

Further Information

Websites:

www.cat.com
Explore the Caterpillar website to see some of the machines in this book, and hundreds of other cool machines.

http://www.seattletimes.com/seattle-news/transportation/berthacam-watch-the-giant-boring-machine-emerge-at-end-of-highway-99-tunnel/
Watch a video of 'Bertha' breaking through the final bit of rock as she finishes tunnelling under Seattle, USA.

http://www.demolitionnews.com/2012/08/17/video-twinkletoes-tackles-stack/
Watch a video of 'Twinkle Toes' and her giantcrusher claw in action, demolishing a chimney.

BOOKS

Mechanic Mike's Machines: Diggers by David West (Franklin Watts)
Machines at Work: Diggers and Cranes by Clive Gifford (Franklin Watts)
Working Wheels: Digger by Annabel Savery (Franklin Watts)

PLACES to VISIT

Diggerland
There are five Diggerland sites in the UK. They are located in Devon, Durham, Kent, Worcestershire and Yorkshire.
www.diggerland.com

Threlkeld Quarry and Mining Museum
This quarry was opened in the 1870s. Today the museum has lots of old digging and mining machines on display and you can take a train ride inside the mine, too.
www.threlkeldquarryandminingmuseum.co.uk

Mining Memorial Museum
This museum in Ohio, USA has the actual bucket that was attached to 'Big Muskie'. You can climb the steps to stand inside it if you are lucky enough to visit.
www.noblecountyohio.com/muskie.html

quarry a large, deep pit where materials, such as coal, are dug from

remote a place, such as a forest or desert, which is far away from places that most people live

reverse to go backwards

track a loop of metal plates that that some vehicles have instead of wheels

INDEX

A

amphibious *18, 27*

army *23*

B

boom *7, 9, 10, 11, 15, 16, 20, 21, 28, 29*

breaker *9*

bucket *4, 6, 8, 10, 11, 16, 17, 23, 27, 28, 29*

building site *8, 20*

C

chainsaw *22*

chaintrencher *22–23, 29*

claw *4, 14, 15*

construction site *4*

crusher *15*

D

Diggerland *24–25, 27, 29*

dinosaur *21*

dredging *19*

dump truck *17, 27*

E

excavator *5–8, 10, 111, 14, 16, 18, 20, 26–29*

H

hydraulic *16*

M

machine *4–6, 8, 10–13, 18, 20–23, 25, 26, 28, 29*

military *23*

N

New Zealand *14, 26*

P

pontoon *19*

Q

quarry *11, 17, 26*

R

river *15, 18, 20*

S

sea *20*

shovel *4, 16, 17*

T

track *4, 7, 9, 11, 17, 20, 28*

truck *17, 22, 23, 27*

U

Ukrainian army *23*

underground *12, 28*

underwater *18, 19, 20*

UK *25*

USA *13, 25, 26*

QUIZ ANSWERS

1 An excavator's arm is called a boom.

2 A micro excavator can fit through a doorway that is 70 cm wide.

3 Dragline excavators 'walk' on giant feet, rather than rolling on tracks.

4 It took *Big Bertha* more than four years to dig a tunnel.

5 The high-reach excavator is called *Twinkle Toes*.

6 Digging buckets have teeth that can be taken off and new ones put on when the teeth wear out.

7 An amphibious excavator can float.

8 Long-reach excavator booms have to be super-strong because they are so long.

9 A chain trencher looks like a massive chainsaw.

10 You have to be at least 1 metre tall to ride on *Spindizzy*.